Called

Reflections on the Story of Jonah

by

F.T. Briones

Foreword by
Pastor Bryan Jacobs

To Jonah

Table of Contents

Foreword	i
Introduction	1
Tethered to truth	4
Get up and go	10
Sleeping in the hold	18
Self-identify	26
Non-heroes	32
From almost to certain	38
Keeping your word	44
Regroup and recover	52
Jonah, Henri, and Edward	58
Unfair	64
Stark changes	70
God's will	76

Called
Reflections on the story of Jonah

Foreword

by Pastor Bryan Jacobs

Everyone at some point asks themselves the question, "Why am I here?" We wonder why God has made us, and what purpose He has for our life. Essentially, we are asking, "What is my calling?" Surprisingly, the answers to these questions are not far from us. They are clearly revealed in Scripture. For example, the primary calling of every person on earth is to become a follower of Jesus Christ. The Bible says we are "called by God to be his own holy people" (1 Cor. 1:2, NLT). The Bible further says that God "desires all people to be saved" (1 Tim. 2:4, ESV). God's main calling for you and for me is to accept Jesus Christ as our only Lord and Savior, turning to Him in repentance and faith, and so be saved.

Besides being saved, God's call for your life and mine is made clear in many other places in Scripture. The Bible says, "give thanks in all circumstances, for this is the will of God in Christ Jesus for you." (1 Thess. 5:18, ESV). How often do

Called
Reflections on the story of Jonah

we wonder which direction God wants us to go in life, but neglect to foster a thankful heart in the process? Elsewhere the Bible says, "For this is the will of God, that by doing good you should put to silence the ignorance of foolish people" (1 Pt. 2:15, ESV). God's will is for us to live honorable lives as examples to those who may not know Him. The Bible may not tell us what school to go to or who to marry, but it does tell us what sort of people God wants us to be. If we do that, God will fill in the details. This is why the Bible says, "Delight yourself in the Lord, and he will give you the desires of your heart." (Psalm 37:4, ESV).

This is why I believe Farah's book is so helpful. While we get lost in the details of life that worry us, God focuses on what sort of person we should be. In her reflections on the book of Jonah, Farah makes clear the applications from Jonah's situation to yours and mine. She will help you to understand what sort of person God is calling you to be through her careful handling of God's word. I have known her for years as a member of our church and as a friend, and I have seen firsthand her love for the Lord, for her family, and for others. I hope that in reading Farah's book you too will sense her love for the Lord, as well as her concern for you, the reader. I pray that you will understand your primary call to accept Christ as Lord and Savior, and then to fulfill your calling in life as you joyfully serve Him. I trust that this book will help you to do that.[1]

---

[1] For more, see another helpful book, *Found: God's Will* by John MacArthur.

Called
Reflections on the story of Jonah

Introduction

I have a young niece who at one point in her toddler years became totally entranced by online unboxing videos. What especially got her spellbound were the videos of a lady opening those little plastic eggs to see what kind of toy might be hidden inside. During her squirmy, can't-sit-still-for-more-than-two-seconds stage of development, my niece actually stopped and held her breath in anticipation of what delightful treasure each plastic egg might hold. It may not exactly be the best metaphor but going through the book of Jonah gave me something of a similar experience.

Like me, this may not be the first time you have heard of Jonah or read through this part of scripture. Like my niece watching one of her favorite videos, you may feel like reading another book about Jonah would be like watching someone open a plastic egg, except this one is transparent. You already know what's inside. I would venture a guess and say that in the past, you may have heard a sermon on Jonah and it was one that focused on this biblical character being a reluctant prophet, or it could have even been about how it aligns with

Messianic messages. Those would have been excellent messages, too, but I pray that you may have picked up this book today eagerly expecting something new.

My prayer for you is that each portion of the book of Jonah will be used by God to speak to you in ways that you may have never heard Him speak before, or bring back to your mind priceless lessons which you might have forgotten. May you be delighted to discover as I did while taking time to reflect through each portion of this marvelous book, that the focus truly is *not* on the imperfect prophet, but the spotlight should truly be shone on the perfect God who called him. This same God and Heavenly Father calls you, too, and He has given us the Book of Jonah so that we can discover things that only He can reveal to us when we come with open hearts eagerly listening. You are called by God.

Come now and let's get cracking.

Called
Reflections on the story of Jonah

Called
Reflections on the story of Jonah

Tethered to truth

> [1] *"Now the word of the Lord came to Jonah the son of Amittai, saying,"*
> *Jonah 1:1 ESV*

Called
Reflections on the story of Jonah

Driving to the train station with my son, Jonah, who was heading back to college after winter break, I challenged him to pray a "scary" prayer. I wanted Jonah to ask the Lord to reveal to him the good deeds that God has prepared in advance for him to do, and trust God to help him do it. *"For we are his workmanship, created in Christ Jesus for good works, which God prepared beforehand, that we should walk in them." (Eph. 2:10 ESV)* I told my son that I would be praying this prayer for myself, too, and that we will both trust God to do as He promised-- that He will enable us to do what He calls us to do, and that the end result will be that God gets the glory.

The Book of Jonah in the Old Testament chronicles for us how God called a man to do a specific task, and through the events that followed that calling, God reveals to us timeless truths about Himself and about ourselves. In fact, it opens with a clear and concise introduction of the two main characters in this account— The Lord and Jonah.

God had a special message to the prophet Jonah. Jonah-- whose name in Hebrew means *dove*, was the son of Amittai-- whose name in Hebrew means *truth*. Even in this one short introductory verse, taking a deeper look into these two names, we can already glean truths about God's calling.

First, it is no coincidence that this prophet's name is Jonah -- *dove*, because we can all surely relate to him. For just as God called Jonah, He calls us even though we have a strong tendency and an innate desire to fly away.

Just as doves are known for their powerful, precise flight patterns[2] we often believe that we know exactly where to go and how best to get there. Nonetheless, whether or not we are aware of it or care to acknowledge it, there is a greater power that ultimately directs our flight paths.

Second, I think it is also by divine purpose that Jonah's father's name means *truth*. Once again, this helps drive a point home. As believers in God, we are His children. He is the Truth, and He is our Father. What is the point here then? Is it that truth gives birth to inquiry and a desire for flight? Maybe. But even more importantly, as children of truth, God is the anchor, the flight director, and the tether that

---

[2] https://sciencing.com/characteristics-doves-8686274.html

Called
Reflections on the story of Jonah

---

both allows us to soar, but also keeps us anchored lest we find ourselves lost in our own foolish pride and willful independence.

As a mother of teens heading into adulthood, I am comforted by this assurance that I find in the book of Jonah-- that I need not worry about my children breaking away from me, as long as I know that they call God their Father, and thus are tethered to the Truth. Even now, as I think about how different my son, Jonah, and I may soon become as he continues to discover the world and becomes exposed to differing views from the university, friends, mass media, and the internet, I can't help but wish sometimes that I might still be able to shield him from what I feel to be erroneous, foolish, and even dangerous. But I choose to hold onto the Truth, or rather, I believe the Truth has a hold of us.

Jonah is tethered to the Truth.

We, each of us who have put our faith in God, are tethered to Him, and on this truth we can rest-- assured and secure. In this blessed assurance we can find true freedom to go, to take flight, and accomplish what it is we are called to do, knowing always that at the other end of the tether, we have our Father, who is Truth, holding on to us.

Think: To whom is your life tethered?

Pray: Lord, help me to trust in you, to put my life in your hands, and to rest in the assurance that even when I lose my strength and need to let go, you are still holding me.

Called
Reflections on the story of Jonah

Get up and go

> *² "Arise, go to Nineveh, that great city, and call out against it, for their evil has come up before me." ³ But Jonah rose to flee to Tarshish from the presence of the Lord. He went down to Joppa and found a ship going to Tarshish. So he paid the fare and went down into it, to go with them to Tarshish, away from the presence of the Lord. Jonah 1:2-3 ESV*

Called
Reflections on the story of Jonah

Before our eldest son went off to college, while my husband and I would get things ready in the kitchen in the morning, there were a set of standard questions that he always seemed to ask me in those early hours. Often the questions would include this particular one: *Is Jonah awake?* Whether it was a school day or a weekend, my husband was always keen on making sure that everyone at home was staying on track, not lagging behind, all of us getting ready to be where we need to be -- all of us, including our eldest son, Jonah. Not wanting to just barge into my son's room, I would stand right outside the partition to his room and ask aloud, "*Jonah, are you awake?*" Almost always the reply would come promptly, and so I would know he's getting ready.

God, in the Book of Jonah, seemed to also be concerned about making sure that the Prophet Jonah was awake and listening to His voice when He spoke to him. God told Jonah to *Arise*. Other translations say, "*Get up and go…*" and "*Up on your feet and on your way…*" Just as a father would prod his children to wake up and get going, the Heavenly Father wanted his child and prophet Jonah to get up and be on his way. God said to Jonah, "*Arise… go… and call out.*"

As it was true for Jonah in the Old Testament, it is true for us today. God wants us to *wake up*, to *rise up*, and *speak up*. Words like these are often used by some in the world as a call to a radical cause which usually seeks to impose their own will on others. But in the context of God's call, these words have little to do with our own will, and *all* to do with what God has prepared in advance for us to accomplish for Him. In the Book of Jonah, not only was it time to arise, it was time to do exactly what the Lord had prepared Jonah to do -- to go and speak His message to the audience He has prepared.

It is interesting to note that in this process of Jonah's *calling*, God alone is in control. God prepares the message, He chooses the messenger, and He determines the audience. Truly, when He says that He has called us to do what He has prepared in advance for us to do (Eph. 2:10), there is no doubt that He has truly prepared *everything*. Looking at the even broader picture, God's preparation of His messenger, Jonah, began even from before his birth. Jonah was placed in just the family, just the nation, at just the right time that determined so that when God's call came, Jonah would be truly prepared. When God's call came, all Jonah needed to do was *get up and go*. The same is still true for us today. When God calls us, we can be sure that He has prepared everything in advance for us to do the work. You are where you are right now, at this particular time in your life, because God has prepared you to be able to respond to His call when He says the time is right. How should we respond to such a call?

Sadly, we are often fooled into thinking that we own our destiny-- that we have the moral compass that works just fine without listening to God; that we can determine who should be helped and who should not, whom we should talk to and whom we should not, where we should go, what we should say, how we should spend our money. We forget just who God is, and how even our very breath comes from Him. *You may forget that you are at every moment totally dependent on God.*[3] What a wonderful thing it is then that God and his truth does not depend on whether I believe Him or remember Him. Just as gravity will not let people just float off into space if

---

[3] C.S. Lewis, *Mere Christianity*

they say there is no such thing as gravity or if they forget what it is that keeps them on the ground-- God is God no matter what people believe.

The prophet Jonah succumbed for a moment to the foolishness of thinking that he could choose to get away from the God on whom his very existence depended. We, too, can be foolish in this way. Convincing ourselves that we can get away from God and His call will not change God and His call in our lives. Like Jonah, we can plan our own way-- pay the fare, get in the boat, sleep and travel as far into the opposite direction of where we have been prepared by God to go, but none of it will change God and His plan for our lives. What a scary and frustrating idea this must be to one who is bent on convincing themselves that they can chart the course of their own lives, but to a person who calls God, Father, what a tremendous comfort is this truth.

As parents, we hope to spare our children from ever falling into foolish thinking that we may have ourselves fallen into in our younger years. New thinking and ideas thrown at us from every direction by professors, new acquaintances, and even celebrities -- all seemed so "sophisticated" and "forward-thinking" when we were younger. We didn't want to be branded as narrow-minded and judgmental, and so we embraced whatever "new" ideas there were. Nonetheless, the passing of time and the school of experience have taught us we really ought to have just held on to *one* thing -- Truth.

Think: Consider the circumstances in your life. Are you doing your best, harnessing all that God has given you, staying sensitive to His voice, so that you may be ready at any time to *get up and go* when God calls you?

Pray: Lord, thank you that you have prepared everything for me to be able to do whatever it may be that you would call me to do. I have nothing to fear.

Called
Reflections on the story of Jonah

Sleeping in the hold

⁴ "But the Lord hurled a great wind upon the sea, and there was a mighty tempest on the sea, so that the ship threatened to break up. ⁵ Then the mariners were afraid, and each cried out to his god. And they hurled the cargo that was in the ship into the sea to lighten it for them. But Jonah had gone down into the inner part of the ship and had lain down and was fast asleep. ⁶ So the captain came and said to him, "What do you mean, you sleeper? Arise, call out to your god! Perhaps the god will give a thought to us, that we may not perish."
Jonah 1:4-6 ESV

Called
Reflections on the story of Jonah

Immediately preceding this passage, we see Jonah deciding to go in the opposite direction of where God told Him to go. Jonah buys a ticket to Tarshish, gets on a boat, and proceeds directly down to the hold ("the inner part of the ship" or the cargo hold), and goes to sleep. (v. 2, 3) I so appreciate the detail the Lord included in those two verses to speak to us about ourselves, our natural tendencies, and the consequences of ignoring or denying Him and His calling in our lives. God, through Jonah, seems to hold up a mirror to us so we can see ourselves.

Like the prophet Jonah, we struggle with the natural tendency to not do what we fully know we ought to do. Actually, we often even *want* to do what we know is right. We know the right thing to do is to follow God's leading, but we still decide to do the opposite. The Apostle Paul in the Book of Romans writes about this struggle, saying, "*For I do not understand my own actions. For I do not do what I want, but I do the very thing I hate.*"[4]

---

[4] *Romans 7:15-20 ESV*

If you have experienced this struggle, then you are familiar with the feelings of frustration, defeat, and sadness that come right after. The kind of sadness that comes after going in the opposite direction of where you know God wants you to go is hard to articulate and unpleasant to face. It makes you want to just go someplace you know no one else will be, turn off the lights and just shut out the world. It is no wonder then that Jonah went straight down to the bottom of the ship-- full of cargo so that it doesn't feel empty, but where there are no people who will ask questions about the decisions he's made-- and just go to sleep. The scripture even says that Jonah paid the fare "to go… away from the presence of the Lord." (v.3) Some have asserted that the Prophet Jonah may have been experiencing depression.[5] Hypersomnia (or excessive sleepiness) has been seen as a symptom of atypical depression especially in teens and young adults.[6] So it can indeed be considered a possibility here. That being said, I think that when one feels that he or she is going away from the presence of the Lord, from the presence of the only

---

[5] Bill Thrasher, Commentary on Jonah, The Moody Bible Commentary, p. 1363

[6] https://www.ncbi.nlm.nih.gov/pmc/articles/PMC3621400/

Called
Reflections on the story of Jonah

One who has proven time and again the reality and constancy of His love, one can almost expect that it would not take long for depression to set in. To make matters worse, the more efforts we make in trying to hide from our life-giving and life-sustaining Lord, the more we cause our own soul and physical body to become out of sync and out of control. Going down to the bottom of the ship, for example, was a sure way for Jonah to have no exposure to sunlight which is one of the things that actually help the physical bodies of humans to function properly and helps to manage our moods. Often, we wish to just go away and disappear, when what we really ought to desire is to stand under the brightness of God's truth and bask in the warmth of His presence.

Yet, the Lord remains Lord, no matter what we think. He is all-powerful and everywhere, and to everything that He is, nothing can compare. No will is stronger, no love is greater, no power is mightier than that of the Lord, and all who belong to Him can never be away from His presence. Just like the sun, always, in due time, He makes His presence known, and when He does no one can deny it.

Called
Reflections on the story of Jonah

God hurled a great storm at the sea to remind Jonah that He is Lord and there is nowhere in the world we can be that He is not. And what an awesome God is He, that even in reaching out to His child who had fallen into despair had made Himself known to others and drew them to Him, just as the mariners on the boat who at first did not believe in the one, true, almighty God ended up believing. What greater god is there who can by His mere presence cause men to tremble in fear and cause unbelievers to fall on their knees? What god is there who can use us even at our lowest to show us and others how great and mighty He is? None. There is none like Him.

God's children can fall into feelings of despair. There are times when we wonder when we will ever become the good person to whom being good, wise, and obedient come easy. We get frustrated at how our own thoughts often lead us to doubt if God and His Word remain relevant to our time, our circumstances, or to the people to whom He wants us to reach out to. In those times we look for the quickest way to go and hide and just sleep--denying the call, denying God, denying even our own darkness. But God's love for us is stubborn and strong-- enough to cause a storm that will rouse us to see first, that God is God no matter how deep the despair we may have caused upon ourselves; and second, that He can use even our sad circumstance to call others to Him.

Think: In times of despair, do you go *down to the hold* where there is darkness, or *up on the deck* where there is sunshine?

Pray: Lord, I praise you that any darkness in my life can be banished by your love and light. Help me to always choose to be with you.

----------- ooo  -----------

Called
Reflections on the story of Jonah

Called
Reflections on the story of Jonah

Self-identify

*⁷ And they said to one another, "Come, let us cast lots, that we may know on whose account this evil has come upon us." So they cast lots, and the lot fell on Jonah. ⁸ Then they said to him, "Tell us on whose account this evil has come upon us. What is your occupation? And where do you come from? What is your country? And of what people are you?" ⁹ And he said to them, **"I am a Hebrew, and I fear the Lord, the God of heaven, who made the sea and the dry land."** ¹⁰ Then the men were exceedingly afraid and said to him, "What is this that you have done!" For the men knew that he was fleeing from the presence of the Lord, because he had told them. Jonah 1:7-10 ESV*

Called
Reflections on the story of Jonah

I watched a powerful video of a conservative black woman who interviewed a conservative white Jewish personality, and after listening to what I felt was a terrific discussion I thought to myself, "Wow, this makes me want to update all my social media profiles to identify myself as a conservative!" So, I quickly went to my social media accounts and then, just as quickly as I got there, something inside me caused me to stop and rethink what it really was that I was doing. I paused and realized that I was going to attach a label to myself for the whole world to see, and because of that I needed to be sure that the labels would be accurate and remain true no matter what happens in the world around me. Sadly, many of the labels based on concepts created by man either do not last, or somehow end up changed by historical or political circumstances.

The Prophet Jonah in this passage was asked to identify himself. In answering the questions that the sailors asked of him, Jonah's response was stated not just truthfully, but also clearly and confidently, so that after he said who he was there would be no question in anyone's mind as to his identity. The sailors asked him several questions, and all of them were answered by the one sentence that Jonah uttered in response. *"I am a Hebrew, and I fear the Lord, the God of heaven, who made the sea and the dry land."* Jonah identified himself in relation to God. Given the polytheistic culture he was living in, even the statement of Jonah's nationality is important so that the sailors knew exactly which God he was referring to. The God of the Hebrews, the only God who is true, almighty, creator of everything-- including the storm that was presently causing them to be so afraid-- that is the God of Jonah, and that was all the information needed so that the sailors knew who Jonah was.

We get a clue here from Jonah on the best way to identify ourselves, and that is to say who we are in relation to our God. In doing so, we have the certainty and confidence that our identity is anchored in the unchanging and eternal truth that is God. No matter what has happened in history, or what will yet happen in human society, our identity remains if we belong to God.

Yet, it is important to remember that the certainty and confidence that comes from identifying ourselves in relation to our God brings with it expectations from others on how we ought to live, as people who identify as such. It seems in this passage that the sailors, upon hearing Jonah identify himself, then wonder how it is that Jonah thinks he can get away from the presence of the Lord. Belief comes instantaneously for the sailors as they ask Jonah, "*what have you done?*" Jonah's words stating his belief in the God who created everything, and his actions of trying to escape God's presence seemed to create great cognitive dissonance in the sailors.

Like the prophet Jonah, have your words or actions ever caused others to ask, "*What have you done?*" Do you live in such a way that cause others to ask, if you believe *this*, then why do you do *that*? If we believe God is our provider, why do we worry? If we believe God is all-powerful, why are we afraid? There are many other similar questions that people who observe us may ask.

The simple answer comes from our flawed human nature which has a tendency toward human pride. But what has pride got to do with worry, or fear, or any of the other things contrary to our belief in God? Pride makes us think we know better. Pride makes us want to do things on our own, and in going our own way and depending on ourselves,

Called
Reflections on the story of Jonah

---

we end up forgetting that our identity, and our very lives exist only by the will of our God.

When we are awakened from the sleep of self-reliant pride, jostled by storms that remind us of the only God who has the power to create the storms and calm them, we are once again able to get back on track toward the path where God calls us to go. And in so going, we become witness to how His greatness can make believers out of those who we may have never thought could ever believe.

Think: How do you identify yourself so that people will know who you truly are?

Pray: Lord, teach me to live according to my identity in you, and to guard my heart against self-reliant pride.

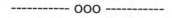

Non-heroes

¹¹ Then they said to him, "What shall we do to you, that the sea may quiet down for us?" For the sea grew more and more tempestuous. ¹² He said to them, "Pick me up and hurl me into the sea; then the sea will quiet down for you, for I know it is because of me that this great tempest has come upon you." ¹³ Nevertheless, the men rowed hard to get back to dry land, but they could not, for the sea grew more and more tempestuous against them. ¹⁴ Therefore they called out to the Lord, "O Lord, let us not perish for this man's life, and lay not on us innocent blood, for you, O Lord, have done as it pleased you." ¹⁵ So they picked up Jonah and hurled him into the sea, and the sea ceased from its raging. ¹⁶ Then the men feared the Lord exceedingly, and they offered a sacrifice to the Lord and made vows.
¹⁷ And the Lord appointed a great fish to swallow up Jonah. And Jonah was in the belly of the fish three days and three nights.
Jonah 1:11-17 ESV

Called
Reflections on the story of Jonah

A real struggle exists in muddling through the grayness of issues that we face in current society. People keep trying to decipher the *"level of goodness"* of one thing over another. In the broken and sad state of our imperfect minds, there seems to reside a perpetual doubt as to the existence of absolutes. Absolute evil and absolute good are always a source of pain and question, especially to those who somehow think their existence was even possible without an absolute God who created them.

Where a person stands on issues such as abortion, for example, tends to hinge on whether or not a person believes in absolute good and evil. And so, we find many lingering in the unstable and stormy gray area that constantly wants to offer "options", assigning "levels of goodness" or validity to the decisions people choose to make on such issues. *Surely*, one might say, *there should be nothing wrong in allowing a woman to decide whether to have a child or not*. Is there not *some good* in trying to make sure that she is better prepared for the responsibility of motherhood, and deciding to terminate the life of the unborn child would be at a *"higher level of goodness"*, or a *"greater good,"* than giving birth to a child who will most likely have a difficult life ahead? It saddens me when I see that this kind of reasoning exists even with those who say they believe in the absolute God. People who reason in this way are like the sailors in this last part of chapter one of the book of Jonah.

The sailors on the ship with Jonah have just been told by him that it is his God, the one true God, the creator of heaven and earth who had created the storm they were currently experiencing. At that moment when they hear and accept this truth, they come to believe and fear the Lord. Nonetheless, their faith still needs to grow in understanding the awesome absolute God. They see His power, and they fear Him. Maybe they fear that they ought not to harm the man of God, and they decide to go against the direct instruction from Jonah to throw him overboard. *Surely*, they may have thought, *it would be a "greater good" to try to save this man's life than to throw him into the sea where he will most likely die*. It is a kind of "heroic" reasoning that we often see portrayed in movies. Whether or not they were trying to be heroes, we see that their initial decision to not follow the direct instruction from Jonah was wrong, and it caused the storm to grow worse.

Called
Reflections on the story of Jonah

But what about Jonah's decision to be thrown overboard? Was he being heroic in his willingness to die rather than to bring harm to the people who were unfortunately on the boat with him? Perhaps in the eyes of the sailors he was. It is also possible that God was speaking to him right then and telling him exactly what he needed to do to stop the storm. However, selfish pride could have also played a part in Jonah's seemingly selfless statement. Based on what happens in the last chapter of the book of Jonah, it is possible that Jonah's main motivation may not have been very heroic. At this point, in his seeming depression, and in the midst of the growing storm reminding him that there is nowhere that he can be away from God's presence, Jonah may have felt so strongly against what God was calling him to do, which is to go to the people of Nineveh, that he may have preferred death over completing the assigned work from God.

Yet, in the growing despair of the events of this first chapter, there emerges a real hero. After the sailors admit the need to obey, and after Jonah is thrown into the sea in the middle of a raging storm, the true hero, God, the creator of everything, commands the storm to cease and literally swoops in to save his child. God commanded a great fish, another one of

Called
Reflections on the story of Jonah

His creations, to swallow Jonah and to later deliver him safely to exactly where he should go.

Why anyone might think they can think better, love better, manage things better than the almighty God is beyond comprehension; and yet we all can fall into being such non-heroes trying our hand at being in control. The storms of life would be so much shorter if only we could keep in mind that man's hubris causes most of man's own misery.

Called
Reflections on the story of Jonah

> ***Think:*** How do you determine where to stand on issues that seem *gray*?
>
> ***Pray:*** Lord, help me to see things through the clarity and certainty of your truth, and to make a stand that shines the light on you.

Called
Reflections on the story of Jonah

From almost to certain

> *Then Jonah prayed to the Lord his God from the belly of the fish, ² saying,*
> *"I called out to the Lord, out of my distress,*
>   *and he answered me;*
> *out of the belly of Sheol I cried,*
>   *and you heard my voice.*
> *³ For you cast me into the deep,*
>   *into the heart of the seas,*
>   *and the flood surrounded me;*
> *all your waves and your billows*
>   *passed over me.*
> *⁴ Then I said, 'I am driven away*
>   *from your sight;*
> *yet I shall again look*
>   *upon your holy temple.'*
> *⁵ The waters closed in over me to take my life;*
>   *the deep surrounded me;*
> *weeds were wrapped about my head*
> *⁶   at the roots of the mountains.*
>   *Jonah 2:1-6a ESV*

Called
Reflections on the story of Jonah

Nothing brings clarity to an uncertain mind and tips the scale from *almost* to *certain* than a close encounter with death. While we know that death eventually comes for each of us, we can only imagine how utterly helpless one must feel standing at death's door and almost stepping through. Suddenly, memories of the past, including the most important decisions made, the people and events that shaped the life that is about to end come flooding back, and in an instant, one realizes what truly mattered most in life. The experience of almost drowning[7], such as what happened to the prophet Jonah after being cast off into the stormy sea, would have had this effect.

In his distress, Jonah prayed to the Lord -- the God whom he knew personally as a child knows his father, whose love has never failed him, yet from whom he tried to get away because in his foolishness he thought his feelings should count more than the calling he received. He may have had feelings of anger for the people of Nineveh, who may have done unimaginable acts of injustice

---

[7] Jonah 2:5

and caused such misery to others and maybe even to himself. Quite understandably, Jonah may have felt that maybe God should choose to just instantly punish these people. Jonah may have felt like King David felt in some of the Psalms where David prayed to God to punish his enemies. Unlike David, however, Jonah was sent by God to a particular people that God has prepared in advance to hear His message which Jonah was to proclaim. Jonah did not want to tell them about the forgiveness and grace that the Father is most willing to give if they chose to repent.

Only by God's grace and power, the storm and sea washed, and cleansed Jonah's thoughts and he called to the Father he knew would not abandon him even when, like a child, he may have acted out in a tantrum or two. And the Father saved Jonah because He is God -- savior, creator, deliverer, sustainer -- and He cannot be anything other than Himself. In an instant, as Jonah may have been almost drowning, he came back to his senses and remembered what mattered most. Through God's mighty intervention, He enabled Jonah to cross over from *almost obeying* to *certainly going* in the direction that he had been called to go. But first, he needed time alone with the Father, and time was given to him in the belly of a big fish.

During stormy days, God quiets my heart and brings me to a place where it is just Him and me. I have no choice but to face my loving Father and ask for forgiveness for my foolish thinking that there can be people who are beyond the reach of His mercy, grace, and unconditional love. People who may have caused hurt and damage to mine and other people's lives knowingly or not. Sometimes there are just things that overwhelm us with feelings of indignation and sorrow and anger, so much so that it sometimes feels like we're going to drown in them. Have you had days like these? Maybe it has been even longer -- weeks, months, years -- perhaps even now, God has gotten a hold of you after a mighty storm in your life and you are ready to admit how you may have gotten things wrong, and how He has always been right.

Called
Reflections on the story of Jonah

Think: Are there people you think are impossible to reach… to love… to forgive?

Pray: Lord, I'm sorry for being so foolish. Focusing only on me when I find it hard to forgive. Thank you for saving me. Please keep working in my life so that I can do what you have prepared for me to do and be what you created me to be.

Called
Reflections on the story of Jonah

Called
Reflections on the story of Jonah

Keeping your word

I went down to the land
  whose bars closed upon me forever;
yet you brought up my life from the pit,
  O Lord my God.
⁷ When my life was fainting away,
  I remembered the Lord,
and my prayer came to you,
  into your holy temple.
⁸ Those who pay regard to vain idols
  forsake their hope of steadfast love.
⁹ But I with the voice of thanksgiving
  will sacrifice to you;
what I have vowed I will pay.
  Salvation belongs to the Lord!"
¹⁰ And the Lord spoke to the fish, and it vomited Jonah out upon the dry land.
Jonah 2:6b-10 ESV

Called
Reflections on the story of Jonah

When young parents or soon-to-be moms and dads ask my husband and I for parenting tips, what most quickly comes to our minds as the most important thing we have learned is this: Always keep your word. Say what you mean and mean what you say. Of course, human frailty will sometimes make this difficult to do, not just as parents but even just as individuals, but it is worth all the effort we can give. We know without a doubt that keeping our word to our children is an indispensable element in making us parents whom our children know they can fully trust and willingly obey. When our children were still toddlers, we agreed that we would never try to make a "quick escape" from the children. We saw other parents do this with their children when we were younger. To avoid having their children cry when they leave, they would have someone distract their child while they quickly "escaped" without the child knowing they had gone. We felt that was not a good way of building a child's trust, and so when it was our turn to have children, we told ourselves we would not do that to them.

While it sometimes broke our hearts a little bit to say goodbye in the first few days that we dropped off our kids at preschool, we would always make sure we said our proper goodbyes and told them that we would come to pick him up at the end of their school day. Our children quickly learned that tearful goodbyes at preschool were totally unnecessary because mom and dad always came back just as they said they would. From that simple, consistent exercise of keeping our word, our children grew up with the assurance that when we say something, we mean it. To them, we never have to say "I promise" when we say we will do something, because they know that when we say we will, we will. Of course, there have been a few times when circumstances made it difficult and even impossible for us to do exactly what we said we would. In those times, we told them why things just couldn't work out the way we had originally planned. We apologized when we failed to keep our word, and we did our best to remedy anything that needed to be remedied. All in all, we have seen how keeping our word is truly one of the most effective and important parenting tools that every mom and dad should have. Through it a child learns to trust, and in whatever circumstance, to also keep their own word to others-- also known as *having integrity*.

Called
Reflections on the story of Jonah

The prophet Jonah learned integrity from his Heavenly Father, and as the Lord's prophet, he had proclaimed His word and spoke of Him to many people. Jonah knew God intimately, probably as children know their parents if not even more intimately, and at the darkest moments when he came close to death, he called out to his Heavenly Father and he was heard.[8] At the moment he realized his foolishness Jonah also remembered that at some point he had made a vow. As a prophet of God, Jonah gave his word to proclaim whatever message the Lord gave him to proclaim. Jonah remembered that he needed to keep his vow, to maintain his integrity, just as he had learned from the Father through his intimate relationship with Him. Jonah knew that he had to keep his word because integrity keeps things together. Literally and figuratively, without integrity things fall apart.

Remembering how the Father has always kept His word, and with much thankfulness for the undeserved love and forgiveness he received from the Lord, Jonah prayed, *"...I'm worshipping you,*

---

[8] Jonah 2:7

Called
Reflections on the story of Jonah

God, calling out in thanksgiving! And I'll do what I promised I'd do!"[9] As Jonah remembered his vow, he also remembered the sure and steadfast integrity of his Father. Just as a child must feel as he sees his dad coming to pick him up just as he said he would, what a comfort it must have been at that very moment for Jonah to remember all the times in the past when God said to him that he would do something and he saw firsthand how God kept His word-- Every. Single. Time. At that point, every bit of doubt he might have had at the beginning, must have disappeared like a puff of smoke, as Jonah proclaimed in his heart, *"Salvation belongs to God!"* As a child might say, *"my dad said he would so he will!"* And as Jonah proclaimed this truth, the Father saved him from the darkness and brought him to exactly where he should be.

Jonah received his calling early in his life, and he responded to it most likely with excitement-- just as we might have felt when we first started getting an inkling of what we might be called to do; maybe something we're good at and somehow makes us feel most useful in making the world a better place.

---

[9] Jonah 2:9, *The Message*

But the loud noises around us and the pride within us sometimes makes us forget Who it is who called, what it is we promised, and how everything was already prepared in advance for us to do what we said we would.

Think: How have you seen God's faithfulness in your life? How do those circumstances show you how you ought to respond when God calls you?

Pray: Thank you Lord for always being true, for showing me what integrity looks like, and giving me the grace that I need so that I can also keep my word.

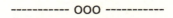

Called
Reflections on the story of Jonah

Called
Reflections on the story of Jonah

Regroup and recover

Then the word of the Lord came to Jonah the second time, saying, ² "Arise, go to Nineveh, that great city, and call out against it the message that I tell you." ³ So Jonah arose and went to Nineveh, according to the word of the Lord. Now Nineveh was an exceedingly great city, three days' journey in breadth ⁴ Jonah began to go into the city, going a day's journey. And he called out, "Yet forty days, and Nineveh shall be overthrown!" ⁵ And the people of Nineveh believed God. They called for a fast and put on sackcloth, from the greatest of them to the least of them.
Jonah 3:1-5 ESV

Called
Reflections on the story of Jonah

Each person has been placed on this earth by God, our Creator, for a reason. To some, the answer to the question of what it is exactly we are called to do remains a mystery. I think of high school juniors and seniors, filling out college application forms and trying to make their best guess as to what course they should take in college, and what career they should be pursuing. As a mom to individuals in this stage in their lives, and having gone through this seemingly excruciating exercise myself, I know that the question, *"what exactly am I called to do or to become?"* can result in sleepless nights.

From the beginning of the Book of Jonah, the prophet had already received clear directions from God as to what his assignment was. We can assume from the text that Jonah had in the past made a vow to be God's prophet. He grew up learning about God and he had a personal relationship with God which firmly assured him of his calling. However, Jonah found this particular assignment hard to do, and he thought he could run away from it and from his Lord. Because of this, God had to intervene in a mighty way, with a storm to wake up Jonah, and a big fish to rescue him and

Called
Reflections on the story of Jonah

---

give him a chance for some quiet reflection as the Lord brought him back on track. He remembered his calling, his vow, and his Lord who has never failed him. He realized that he failed in this assignment, but he knows that God forgives and will mercifully get him back up on his feet again.

I picture God in this passage with Jonah to be like a dad who helps his son who may have fallen down on the ground on his way to a goal. The dad would wipe away the child's tears, maybe give his son a reassuring hug, and then remind his son what it was that he was aiming to do before he fell. God repeats the assignment to Jonah and gives Jonah another chance to respond. Jonah, having learned from his fall and being reassured of the Father's faithfulness and forgiveness, takes this second chance and goes directly to do what he ought to have done in the first place.

Like Jonah, we must also take the time to regroup in order to recover if we have failed or lost our way. What a joy and reassurance it is to know that our Heavenly Father will help us even in such times of failing and getting back up. He will remind us what we are called to do, and He will enable us to do it.

Called
Reflections on the story of Jonah

Whether it takes a storm and a big fish to bring us back, God will do it because He is God and we, His children, are never too far or out of reach of His love and grace. As our Father, it pleases Him to see His children, after having fallen, pick ourselves up, ask for forgiveness, and *try again*. Yet, it pleases Him when we finally realize that we cannot do it on our own. We need Him. In everything that He calls us to do -- in big things such as career choice, or in everyday things such as making wise and godly decisions -- we need Him.

Jonah helps us to see here that doing what we are called to do may include times of failing, getting up, and trying again; however, ultimately realizing that we need God's help. C.S. Lewis states this point well. He wrote, *"Now we cannot...discover our failure to keep God's law except by trying our very hardest (and then failing). Unless we really try, whatever we say there will always be at the back of our minds the idea that if we try harder next time, we shall succeed in being completely good. Thus, in one sense, the road back to God is a road of moral effort, of trying harder and harder. But in another sense, it is not trying that is ever going to bring us home. All this trying leads up to the vital moment at which you turn to God and say, 'You must do this. I can't.'"*[10]

---

[10] C.S. Lewis, *Mere Christianity*

Think: God calls us everyday to live for Him, and He is the only one who can help us do so consistently. If you have given your heart to Him and have seen Him work in your everyday life, you can be sure that He will enable you to be all that He calls you to be.

Pray: Thank you Lord that in all my tryings and failings you reveal to me the power and strength I have in you.

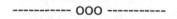

Called
Reflections on the story of Jonah

Jonah, Henri, and Edward

The word reached the king of Nineveh, and he arose from his throne, removed his robe, covered himself with sackcloth, and sat in ashes. ⁷ And he issued a proclamation and published through Nineveh, "By the decree of the king and his nobles: Let neither man nor beast, herd nor flock, taste anything. Let them not feed or drink water, ⁸ but let man and beast be covered with sackcloth, and let them call out mightily to God. Let everyone turn from his evil way and from the violence that is in his hands. ⁹ Who knows? God may turn and relent and turn from his fierce anger, so that we may not perish."
¹⁰ When God saw what they did, how they turned from their evil way, God relented of the disaster that he had said he would do to them, and he did not do it.
Jonah 3:6-10 ESV

Called
Reflections on the story of Jonah

Do you sometimes think about whether or not it matters what you do? At the beginning of the book of Jonah, it seemed like he might not have given this question much thought. Did he wonder what consequences may come out of his stubborn disobedience? Besides preventing the people of Nineveh from hearing the message from the Lord, do you think Jonah may have thought that his disobedience could have even greater consequences? And when he finally decided to obey, could he have imagined how great an impact his own actions may cause?

Thinking about the consequences of our actions makes me consider the work of two men in more recent history, mathematicians Henri Poincare and Edward Lorenz. Poincare and Lorenz are the originators of Chaos Theory. In summary, *"Chaos theory is a mathematical theory that can be used to explain complex systems such as weather, astronomy, politics, and economics. Although many complex systems appear to behave in a random manner, chaos theory shows that, in reality, there is an underlying order that is difficult to see.*"[11] It is from Lorenz's famous talk on Chaos Theory in relation to weather patterns that the term "*butterfly effect*" came about. His talk was entitled, "*Predictability: Does the Flap of a Butterfly's Wings in Brazil set off a Tornado in Texas?*"

At first glance, it may have looked like Jonah's response to his calling would mainly affect only himself. Yet, as the story unfolds, we see how his every response results in something much greater than what he may have initially thought. His decision to go to sleep in the cargo hold of a ship headed in the opposite direction of where he was supposed to go had so far caused a great storm, a near-death experience for him and other people, and the appearance of a big fish in which he spent three days and found himself renewed in his commitment to the Lord.

As the story progresses in chapter 3, Jonah sees that his obedience is causing changes in the people around him. The people of Nineveh believed in God[12], and even more than that, the King of

---

[11] https://www.learning-theories.com/chaos-theory.html
[12] Jonah 3:5

Nineveh himself heard the message and not just believed, but repented, and told all of Nineveh to also repent. The great king of this polytheistic nation, heard the message, chose to believe in Jonah's one true God, and sent out a decree saying *"Let everyone turn from his evil way and from the violence that is in his hands."*[13] Jonah's decision to obey caused a king and his people to believe and repent. Can there still be doubt that one person's decision, especially in relation to God's calling, can cause greater events to occur which is far beyond what that person ever could have imagined?

Poincare and Lorenz recognized that human vision and understanding are so limited that we often fail to see that there is order in the seeming chaos that we see around us. Many people choose to think that things just happen randomly. But even mathematicians recognize that there is order -- that everything needs to be somehow held in place, because even a slight change can have dramatic ramifications. The Bible shows us the Divine Hand that truly holds everything in place so that the world is not thrown into chaos, and here, in the book of

---

[13] Jonah 3:8

Called
Reflections on the story of Jonah

Jonah, we see a demonstration of how one person's choice can have a tremendous effect.

Think: How have you seen seemingly small things cause big things to happen in your life? How does this affect your decision-making?

Pray: Lord, thank you for the assurance that even in seeming chaos, I can trust in the assurance that you hold everything-- the world, my life, my future-- in your hands.

Unfair

But it displeased Jonah exceedingly, and he was angry. ² And he prayed to the Lord and said, "O Lord, is not this what I said when I was yet in my country? That is why I made haste to flee to Tarshish; for I knew that you are a gracious God and merciful, slow to anger and abounding in steadfast love, and relenting from disaster. ³ Therefore now, O Lord, please take my life from me, for it is better for me to die than to live." ⁴ And the Lord said, "Do you do well to be angry?" ⁵ Jonah went out of the city and sat to the east of the city and made a booth for himself there. He sat under it in the shade, till he should see what would become of the city.
Jonah 4:1-5 ESV

Called
Reflections on the story of Jonah

In a family of siblings close in age, I remember how my mother would often try to make sure that none of us ever sensed any favoritism among us, her children. Now as adults though, when we would get together for family gatherings, we would tease each other and our mom, making guesses as to who the real favorite child was based on shared memories from years long past. I sometimes catch myself during these conversations wondering how my own children's future conversations might go when they are older. Parents who love and care for their children, certainly know how important showing fairness is in being able to minimize hurt and conflict among their children. So as parents, we try our best to be fair, but one way or another, children can have a knack for still perceiving things to be unfair even when it is not.

The prophet Jonah cried, "*Unfair!*" to the Heavenly Father, when he saw that the people he only knew as evil were not getting the punishment he thought they deserved. Jonah even went as far as saying, "*I knew it!*", telling God that he didn't want to follow God's calling in the first place because He knew

Called
Reflections on the story of Jonah

---

that God is gracious and merciful, and that people who repent and ask for forgiveness will indeed be forgiven by the Father. In a twisted sort of way, Jonah's personal relationship with the Father helped him make an accurate prediction of what would happen, but it seems he did not learn enough from this personal relationship to understand that God's forgiveness of the people is truly what fairness looks like. How could he say that God's mercy toward the people of Nineveh was unfair when he had so recently experienced mercy and forgiveness himself? And so, God said to Jonah, *"What do you have to be angry about?"*[14]

Based on what we have established from Jonah's behavior in the earlier chapters, it is not surprising to see his response to God's question. When asked to confront and think through his complaint, hurt, and anger, Jonah just leaves. Like his decision in the first chapter to leave and just go someplace where he can sleep and not have to face the realities of his life, Jonah just turns and leaves. A parent's first instinct toward an adult child who does

---

[14] Jonah 4:4, *The Message*

what Jonah did might be to say, "*Don't you see that you're the one being unfair? I have always been here for you. Listening to you. Rescuing you. Forgiving you. Loving you. Now I'm talking to you and you just walk away?*"

Like Jonah, we all too often tend to choose to only see things the way we've initially judged things to be. Many times, we see people and things going on around us and we make a choice about how we think things should turn out, and how we ought to treat such people or situations going forward. Yet God shows us such radical things as grace, mercy, and forgiveness which ought to alter the way to respond yet we choose to just leave instead of confronting things and admitting where our flawed reasoning has led us astray.

Thankfully, our Heavenly Father understands us perfectly. In His perfect wisdom and love He chooses to pursue us even in those times when our pride causes us to leave and go our own way. Truly, God's perfect love saves us from such hurts caused by our own folly.

Think: Has God revealed errors in judgements you may have made about people or situations in your life? Will you stay and deal with the matter in your heart with God?

Pray: Lord, please reveal to me any areas in my life where I may be blinded by my own anger or erroneous judgement and help me to stay and see things through your eyes.

Called
Reflections on the story of Jonah

Stark changes

"⁶Now the Lord God appointed a plant and made it come up over Jonah, that it might be a shade over his head, to save him from his discomfort. So Jonah was exceedingly glad because of the plant. ⁷ But when dawn came up the next day, God appointed a worm that attacked the plant, so that it withered. ⁸ When the sun rose, God appointed a scorching east wind, and the sun beat down on the head of Jonah so that he was faint. And he asked that he might die and said, "It is better for me to die than to live." ⁹ But God said to Jonah, "Do you do well to be angry for the plant?" And he said, "Yes, I do well to be angry, angry enough to die." ¹⁰ And the Lord said, "You pity the plant, for which you did not labor, nor did you make it grow, which came into being in a night and perished in a night. ¹¹ And should not I pity Nineveh, that great city, in which there are more than 120,000 persons who do not know their right hand from their left, and also much cattle?"
Jonah 4:6-11 ESV

Called
Reflections on the story of Jonah

Sometimes changes in our lives are so stark that we feel they merit nothing short of our most dramatic responses. The Book of Jonah ends in such a manner, or so it seems to the prophet whose response to his calling has brought him through an epic experience. From quiet slumber in the bottom of a ship, to waking up to a raging storm and a near-death experience. From three days in the darkness of the belly of a big fish, to landing on the shores of Nineveh-- the place where he did not want to go. From proclaiming disaster to the people he thought deserved punishment, to seeing the same people repent and believe in God. From being happy about God's forgiveness of his own disobedience, to being angry that God will forgive others. The night and day differences that we find in this account of Jonah's tumultuous journey to complete the task he was called by God to do are many, but they so aptly reflect what we may also experience in our own lives.

Jonah told God it was unfair of Him to hold back on destroying Nineveh, the land whose people Jonah found so despicable that God's forgiveness of them made him feel like it was better for him to die than to see them spared. Jonah could not see the irony of his statements and his sentiments. Like a child

Called
Reflections on the story of Jonah

---

throwing a tantrum, his present rush of emotions prevented him from clearly seeing his own past and present experience of forgiveness from God. Not only had he been personally forgiven by God, and just recently experienced the awesome power of God, and the lengths God will go to reach and save him, but he has seen how God has forgiven his own people time and time again throughout his nation's history. Yet God, all-powerful, all-wise, abounding in grace, mercy, and love, takes the time to teach Jonah in a way that only He can do it. God reaches out to Jonah in a way that He knows Jonah will understand. Just as a father who has built a strong relationship with his child will know exactly how to make their child understand what they are trying to say, God took the time to put together an object lesson for Jonah.

By commanding a plant, a worm, and even the sun to interact with Jonah at this particular point in his life, God delivered a clear message of his power, his wisdom, his mercy, and his love to his child. And allowing us to have the Book of Jonah in our hands for us to read and study, God reaches out to us as well. Beyond the invaluable lessons of God's forgiveness and mercy to all who listen to His message and choose to repent, just as what happened to the people and land of Nineveh, other golden nuggets of truth can be unearthed here, especially as it relates to God and his children:

1. **God loves and knows His children personally.** Just as He loved and knew Jonah on a personal level, God knew how best to reach Jonah and help him overcome the obstacles that lay in his way to doing what he was called to do (even when the obstacle was Jonah himself), God knows and loves you and me in this way, too.

2. **There is no limit to how God can choose to save his children and to show just how much He loves each one.** All of nature is within God's control, and he can and does use nature to reach His children with his message. And even more than this, God chose to give Himself to save us. *"... God shows His love for us in that while we were still sinners, Christ died for us."*[15]

3. **Accomplishing what we are called to do can only be done with God's help.** Jonah,

---

[15] Romans 5:8 ESV

even with all the training, guidance, education and discipline he must have acquired while growing up, still could accomplish what he was called to do *only* through the power of God. Without God's power, even our best efforts can still come to nothing.

4. **Finding joy in our calling only comes in seeing things through God's perspective, and only God can help us see things this way.** God could have just left Jonah to sulk in the end, but God saw it necessary to teach His child a lesson so that he can fully understand and find joy in seeing the big picture and how his calling fit within it.

Think: What have you learned personally about yourself and God as you read and studied the Book of Jonah?

Pray: Lord, thank you for the Book of Jonah and for how, through your Word, I can learn more about how you call me and care for me in a very personal way.

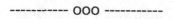

Called
Reflections on the story of Jonah

God's will

As you've reached the end of this book, I guess you might be asking, "What is it that God calls me to do? What exactly is God's will for my life?"

Pastor Bryan Jacobs spoke to our church's youth group one weekend and gave them a message to tell them once and for all what God's will is for their lives. No, he did not tell them what they should major in when they go to college, or what career path each of them should pursue. He told them they are actually free to do what they want if they live according to God's will. Pastor Bryan summarized God's will, as shown in God's word, into 6 key words that all start with the letter S to help make them easier to remember.

God's will is for you to be:

1. Saved –
"³ This is good, and it is pleasing in the sight of God our Savior, ⁴ who desires all people to be saved and to come to the knowledge of the truth."
1 Timothy 2:3-4 ESV,

"The Lord is not slow to fulfill his promise as some count slowness, but is patient toward you, not wishing that any should perish, but that all should reach repentance."
2 Peter 3:9 ESV

2. Spirit-filled –

"[17] Therefore do not be foolish, but understand what the will of the Lord is. [18] And do not get drunk with wine, for that is debauchery, but be filled with the Spirit, [19] addressing one another in psalms and hymns and spiritual songs, singing and making melody to the Lord with your heart, [20] giving thanks always and for everything to God the Father in the name of our Lord Jesus Christ, [21] submitting to one another out of reverence for Christ."
Ephesians 5:17-21

3. Submissive –

"[13] Be subject for the Lord's sake to every human institution, whether it be to the emperor as supreme, [14] or to governors as sent by him to punish those who do evil and to praise those who do good [15] For this is the will of God, that by doing good you should put to silence the ignorance of foolish people."
1 Peter 2:13-15 ESV

4. Sanctified –

"³ For this is the will of God, your sanctification: that you abstain from sexual immorality; ⁴ that each one of you know how to control his own body in holiness and honor, ⁵ not in the passion of lust like the Gentiles who do not know God; ⁶ that no one transgress and wrong his brother in this matter, because the Lord is an avenger in all these things, as we told you beforehand and solemnly warned you. ⁷ For God has not called us for impurity, but in holiness. ⁸ Therefore whoever disregards this, disregards not man but God, who gives his Holy Spirit to you."
1 Thessalonians 4:3-8 ESV

5. Suffering –

"For it is better to suffer for doing good, if that should be God's will, than for doing evil."
1 Peter 3:17 ESV

"Therefore let those who suffer according to God's will entrust their souls to a faithful Creator while doing good."
1 Peter 4:19 ESV

6. Saying thanks –

"give thanks in all circumstances; for this is the will of God in Christ Jesus for you."
1 Thessalonians 5:18 ESV

Stay in God's will and He will mold your heart to want to do the things that please Him and that will show you without a doubt that He is the one who calls you, who hears you, and who loves you like no other.

Made in the USA
Las Vegas, NV
03 October 2023